ITALIAN ARTILLERY 1914-1945 Vol. 1

65/17, 75/13, 75/27, 77/28, 100/17, 105/28, FIAT 20B AND PAVESI P4 TRACTOR

LUCA STEFANO CRISTINI

BOOK SERIES FOR MODELLERS & COLLECTORS

CONTENTS

▲ Artillery company with 65/17 piece in AOI in 1935.

THE WEAPONS ENCYCLOPÆDIA

TANK AIRCRAFT AFV SHIP ARTILLERY VEHICLES SECRET WEAPON

TWE-006 ENG

ITALIAN ARTILLERY 1914-1945

THE WEAPONS ENCYCLOPAEDIA

PUBLISHED BY

Luca Cristini Editore (Soldiershop), via Orio, 35/4 - 24050 Zanica (BG) ITALY.

DISTRIBUTION BY

Soldiershop - www.soldiershop.com, Amazon, Ingram Spark, Berliner Zinnfigurem (D), LaFeltrinelli, Mondadori, Libera Editorial (Spain), Google book (eBook), Kobo, (eBoook), Apple Book (eBook).

PUBLISHING'S NOTES

LICENSES COMMONS

CONTRIBUTORS OF THIS VOLUME & ACKNOWLEDGEMENTS

We thank the main contributors to this issue: Enrico Finazzer & Carlo Cucut. The profiles of the tanks are all by the author. Photo coloring by Anna Cristini. Special thanks to national and/or private institutions such as: Army General Staff, State Archives, Bundesarchiv, Nara, Library of Congress, etc. To P. Crippa, A.Lopez, L.Manes, C.Cucut, Tallillo archives, for making available images or other of their archives.
Special thanks to "Minstrel" who edited the corrections of the English text.

For a complete list of Soldiershop titles, or for every information please contact us on our website: www.soldiershop.com or www. cristinieditore.com. E-mail: info@soldiershop.com. Keep up to date on Facebook & Twitter: https://www.facebook.com/soldiershop. publishing

Title: **ITALIAN ARTILLERY 1914-1945 VOL. 1** Code.: **TWE-006 EN**
Series edited by a L. S. Cristini
ISBN code: 978-88-93278874. First edition October 2022
THE WEAPONS ENCYCLOPAEDIA (SOLDIERSHOP) trademark of Luca Cristini Editore

INTRODUCTION

During the Second World War, Italy suffered from a lack of modern artillery pieces that could have made a difference, giving much needed support to their ground forces. The reasons for this situation were to be found in a very curious series of factors. The first of these was due to the nation's recent history, Italy had emerged victorious from the First World War, and consequently the nation acquired a considerable amount of former Austro-Hungarian guns and howitzers, which had been captured by Italian forces in their successful offensive action in the last stage of the War and as part of the war reparations imposed on the defeated enemy. This was in the main, good-quality material, for it's time and had been produced by some of the best factories in Europe, such as the Bohemian Skoda and Bohler. Arising from this unexpected 'inheritance', the planners in the Italian Army did not feel the need to develop and adopt anything new for many years.

Another factor was the deficient national economy, a factor that accompanied the Italian armed forces throughout the period up to the end of the Second World War. The dictatorship then in power sought, by military adventures, to seal its international prestige, although this was more a bluff than a 'true' reality. In fact, the Abyssinian adventures and later intervention in Spain alongside the Nationalist military, did nothing but deplete the treasury and heavily affected preparations for the approaching conflict.

Finally, the short-sighted strategic vision of the General Staff of the time was a key factor in the lack of preparedness. The Italian mountainous border was thought to be the only real front exposed to possible future wars, and consequently strategic issues relating to, for example, the colonies were neglected. Therefore, particular weight was given to the study and production of modern but light artillery pieces, ignoring medium or heavy pieces, and as such the Ansaldo industrial firm were requested to improve, where possible, the guns received as booty from Austrian reparations.

During the war, attempts were made to remedy this deficit to some extent, but the Italian armed forces had by then fallen far behind both their opponents and allies.

In this and the next two volumes on the subject, we will not deal with tracked armoured artillery, which will be published in dedicated texts. However these volumes will examine (with trailing pieces, cannons, guns, howitzers and bombards) the types and uses of towed artillery used in the Second World War, including those in service from the Great War to those made afterwards. We will also include the tractors and prime movers used to move the pieces, in the appendix.

▲ 100/17 (ex Skoda) at the Rocca in Bergamo. Photo by the author.

■ ADAPTATION OF OLD GUNS

The work carried out byAnsaldo-Fossati was extensive starting in the early post-war period. Initially, it was planned to settle the issue of towing the pieces, which had traditionally been carried out by animals, but the First World War had caused serious losses to suitable stock and the growth in more reliable internal combustion engines offered new opportunities.

Artillery pieces moved by animal power had traditionally been mounted on wooden wheels, and towing them over uneven terrain was very hard on the mechanisms of the guns. In the light of experience from the First World War, one of the first tasks that needed to be done as soon as possible was to provide the guns with modern tractors and tyred wheels to ensure faster, safer and less wearing movement. Initially a limber between cannon and tractor called an elastic bogie was devised, with metal and rubber wheels, which solved the problem to some extent.

As war approached, a programme was initiated to replace the original wooden wheels with new metal wheels, first in "elektron "(a type of ultra-light alloy consisting of magnesium and aluminium) and later in the stronger pressed steel. This improved the operational use of the pieces considerably, as they allowed them to be towed directly by artillery tractors, but economic and organisational problems typical of Italian military production at that time resulted in long lead times, and by June 1940, only a few dozen guns had been uprated in accordance with the modernisation directives.

Other improvements were made to ammunition performance and solutions were devised to ensure longer ranges and penetration capabilities. A good result was achieved with the new hollow charge shells, the EP and EPS, which gave good anti-tank performance.

In the case of devising suitable tractors, the focus was mainly on vehicles for towing heavy artillery pieces. In this respect, some very interesting solutions were developed with vehicles that continued their operational life until the mid-1950s. On the other hand, animals were still used extensively, as was also the case in the German army. It was also common for Italian units to use suitable commercial and private vehicles for towing the lighter pieces.

▲ Front view of a 75/27 on display at the Parco delle Rimembranze in the Rocca of Bergamo. Photo by author.

▲ A 105/28 in battery on the Cyrenaic front, North Africa, 1942. State Archives.

▲ A well-known image from June 1940. In the absence of mules, Alpine troops are also useful for the transport of this 75/13 cannon.

▲ A 100/17 Mod. 14 in action in the first battle of the Tembien.

■ THE PRE-WAR SITUATION

Given the vital importance of the artillery arm it was not until March 1940 that the General Staff were ordered to compile a plan for the renewal and replacement of the obsolete artillery still in service, a considerable delay in the modernisation program begun in the 1920's.

The main proposal was to produce replacement for the World War 1 era artillery, which had already been defined and officially adopted since 1935 with the 75/18, 149/40 and the 210/22 models but of which very few had been produced until then, and adopt other even more recent weapons (the 105/40, 149/19 and the 90/53). The project also envisaged keeping in service those old types of artillery that could still provide useful service, such as the 75/13 Someggiato, and the 100 model in various types the latter would demonstrate an unexpected vitality by remaining in service for several years after the conflict.

In total the plan was involved in putting no less than 15,000 new guns of all calibres into production, and also providing sufficient ammunition for them. To finance this, an expenditure of approximately 17 billion lire was planned for 1940!

This project was far beyond even the most optimistic expectations, in fact nothing came of it. Everything was lacking: money, raw materials and an industrial base suitable for realisation with the necessary work force for mass production at this level.

In the end, they were content to make a modest number of 149/40 and 210/22 pieces, but also a few 75/18, 90/53 and 149/19 pieces, with the result that the Regio Esercito arrived on 8 September with old artillery, much of it dating back to the First World War.

On the eve of the Second World War, the Artillery Regiment began to grow again and by June 1940, there were 54 field regiments, 3 'Celeri', 5 Alpine divisions, 18 corps, 5 army divisions, 6 Frontier Guards, 2 armoured, 5 anti-aircraft and 2 motorised regiments in the Italian Royal Army. After the armistice of 1943, the 11th 'Legnano', 184th 'Nembo', 7th 'Cremona', 35th 'Friuli', 152nd 'Piceno' and 155th 'Mantova' regiments the remnants were formed into both the 1st Motorised Regiment and the Italian Liberation Corps and Combat Groups.

ORGANISATION OF THE ARTILLERY

The main armament of the Regio Esercito at the start of the new conflict consisted of the following:

- **Regimental level** (a few pieces per type): a battery of 65/17 howitzers. A company of 47/32 anti-tank guns of 4 or 8 per section.

- **Divisional level**: an artillery regiment, consisting of 3 groups of 3 batteries of 4 pieces each (based on 2 batteries of 75 and 1 of 100 for each group). There was also a 47/32 gun company for the anti tank role; the main task of the divisional artillery was to counter mobile targets, typically armoured and vehicles in general, and provide a close support function for the infantry.

- **At army corps level:** a heavy artillery grouping on 105 cannons and 149 howitzers; main function counter-battery firing to eliminate or counter enemy artillery. On paper fully motorised, less mobile than divisional units but obviously more powerful.

- **At army level:** grouping of heavy artillery of 140 and 152 guns and howitzers of various calibres. There was also the presence of anti-aircraft defence units. The large pieces available to the army groupings did not require a high level of mobility. It was equipped with the largest calibres, suitable for long-range fire on enemy targets, which were not within the lower units. When needed, it provided counter-battery support to divisional and army sections.

At the date of entry into the war, the Regio Esercito had about 8,000 artillery pieces of all types at its disposal, to which must be added the light pieces, about 1,000 47/32 anti-tank and 700 65/17 mountain howitzers. Of these, only a few hundred were of recent manufacture. The rest of the material dated back to the Great War, and in some cases even to the early 1900s which had been partially modernised.

▲ Artillery components intent on manoeuvring a 75/27 1915-1918.

Once the war had started, the experience gained demonstrated a need for new systems such as self-propelled artillery, particularly in the light of lessons learnt from German experience.

In addition to the aforementioned pieces, the Italian army, in the course of the conflict, also found itself with weapons captured from the enemy, in Africa, Russia or the Balkans, as well as supplies purchased from their German ally.

For those unfamiliar with Italian Artillery numbering the first number is the calibre in mm, the second barrel length as a multiple of the calibre and modello (mod) where mentioned refers to service year introduction. So for example the standard anti-tank gun the 47/32 had a bore of 47mm and a barrel length of 32x47 = 1.504 m. Later increased to 40x47 to fire a more powerful shell. This nomenclature applies to virtually all the artillery pieces mentioned below in the service of The Regio Esercito (The Royal Italian Army).

▲ A 100/17 piece with elektron and rubber wheels, Pontida Shrine. Photo by the author.

THE INHERITANCE FROM THE GREAT WAR

As already announced, this first volume we will deal with artillery pieces produced before or during the First World War, both domestically produced and as a result of war booty mainly of Austro-Hungarian origin from combat in 1915-1918 and as reparations after victory.

The criterion used will be that of increasing calibre, i.e. from light pieces onwards. In the second volume, to be published soon, there will be a complete examination of the ex-WWI pieces, while the third will mainly deal with the more modern guns, designed from the second half of the 1930s onwards. Mortars are planned for the second of these three volumes, while tractors and prime movers will be included throughout the three volumes in chronological order.

In this first volume, we will deal with the following pieces and artillery vehicles:

- **The 65/17 cannon** Mod. 1908-1913. Originated as the 65A mountain cannon.

- **The 75/13 howitzer** Mod. 1915. Austro-Hungarian war booty, manufactured by Skoda.

- **The 75/27 cannon** Mod. 1906-1911. Built under German licence by Krupp from 1911.

- **The 77/28 cannon** Mod. 1905. Austro-Hungarian war booty, manufactured by Böhler.

- **The 100/17 howitzer** Mod. 1914-1916. Austro-Hungarian spoil of war, manufactured by Skoda.

- **The 105/28 cannon** Mod. 1916. Produced by Ansaldo based on a Schneider design.

Artillery tractors and prime movers are included in the appendix:

- **Fiat 20B tractor** Mod. 1916-1920. WWI artillery tractor.

- **Pavesi P4/100 tractor** Mod. 25-26-30 and 30A. Famous domestically produced tractor.

- **Breda TP32 tractor** Mod. 25-26-30 and 30A. Italian heavy artillery tractor.

▲ Beautiful picture of a 65/17 cannon in the Alps during the Great War. Wikipedia cc1

65/17 CANNON WITH PROTECTIVE SHIELD - SPANISH CIVIL WAR 1936-1939

65-17 CANNON

The 65/17 cannon dates from 1911, when the Turin Arsenal was commissioned to study a 65mm-calibre howitzer with the ability to be broken down for transport and would be adopted by the Regio Esercito with the designation Obice 65/17 mod. 1913. Conceived as a mountain cannon (the intention was to equip all Alpine corps as pack artillery, i.e. transported by mules. Once the load was disassembled, it was divided into five parts: barrel - shield - breech block - slide and brake - tail and wheels), it was later universally assigned to infantry regimentsfor close support.

Due to its versatility, it was highly appreciated during the Great War for its ease of operation and the fact that numbers could be easily carried and transported to high altitudes. Its versatility also made it useful as an anti-tank weapon within the fortified works of the Alpine Wall on the Isonzo front, later in Abyssinia, in the Spanish Civil War and in World War II, especially in North Africa, where it was often mounted on the back of lorries.

However, the 65/17 piece was not perfect, the design meant the gun had restricted ability to fire at a high elevation; however many of the available photographs show how troops, thanks to its low weight, obviated this limitation by careful placement of the gun as needed. The piece also had a short range of 6500 metres, with a limited arc of fire, which forced the gunners to get as close as possible to the target. All these shortcomings were partly compensated for by a good rate of fire.

In 1920 it was replaced, as a mountain gun, by the Austrian Škoda 75/13 howitzer, but nevertheless remained in widespread service and was employed in the reconquest of Libya.

SPECIFICATIONS:	
Entry into service	1913
Weight in battery	570 kg
Projectile weight	5 kg
Initial projectile speed	360 m/sec
Horizontal firing sector	8°
Vertical firing sector	-8° / +20°
Maximum range	6.500 metres
Rate of fire	min 6/max 12
Number of pieces available in 1940	719

▲ 65/17 cannon towed by a Moto Guzzi Trialce of the 80th Infantry Division 'La Spezia'. Wikipedia cc1

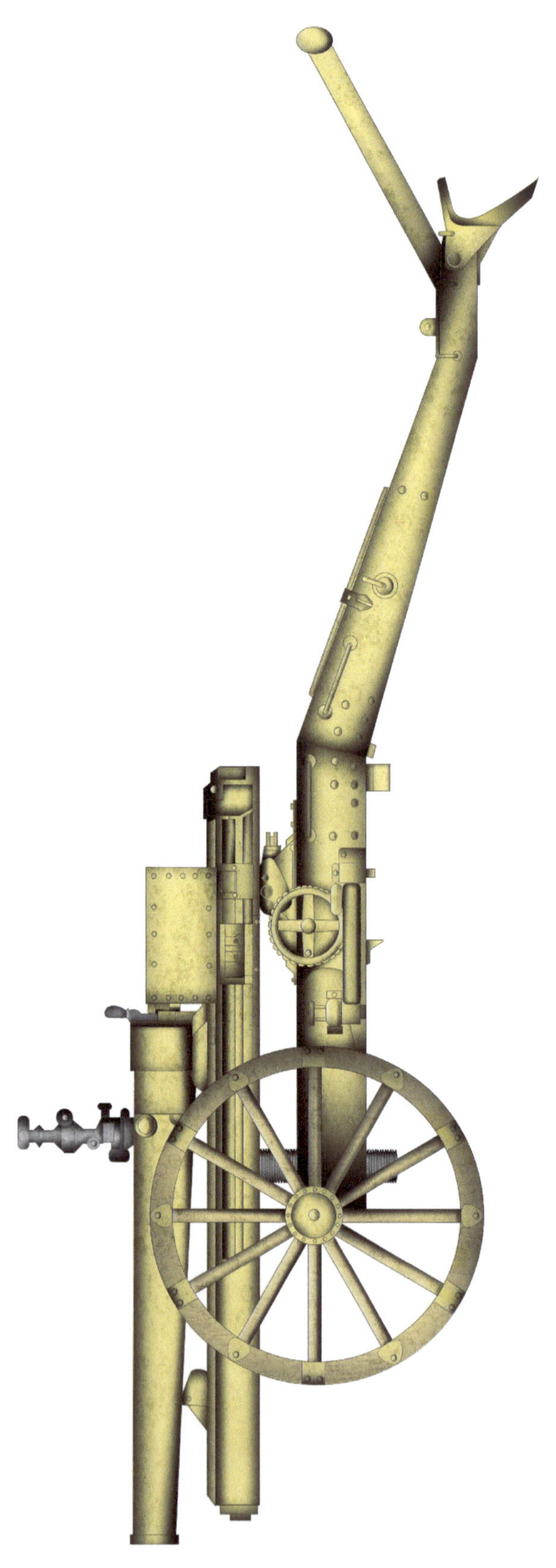

After 1928, the 65/17 was converted into an infantry gun and 200 new examples were distributed, modified from the original, so as to be able to pulled by a horse or a group of soldiers.

However it was intended as soon as possible to produce a replacement with a longer-range weapon, but due to the, usual, lack of resources this was only partially met with the introduction of 75/18 howitzers. In fact, the 65/17 continued to be used mainly on the fronts outside the mainland, particularly in North Africa, Italian East Africa and the Greek front, remaining active until the end of the conflict. It was not employed in Russia.

When it was officially assigned to infantry regiments, these received three per regiment, later increased to four in 1934. During this period, it was also adapted for towing behind a vehicle, with the wooden wheels being replaced by Elektron wheels with solid rubber semi-pneumatics tyres.

However, this last operation was not completed quickly as the pictures from the Abyssinian war show, where it was widely used and where the pieces almost always appear with wooden wheels. In the Ethiopian War, the gun was also assigned to the colonial and divisional artillery groups of the Alpini and Blackshirts.

During the Spanish Civil War, around 350 pieces accompanied the Italian volunteer corps, who in turn distributed them to the Nationalist forces. In this theatre of war, the gun demonstrated good service in an anti-tank role due to the relatively thin armour of the Soviet supplied tanks of the Republicans.

For this specific role, however, in 1935 a dedicated anti- tank gun was introduced, the more modern 47/32, while the remaining guns were assigned to second line units such as the Frontier Guard and Militia batteries. At the outbreak of the Second World War, 719 pieces were still in service, including newly manufactured ones made to replace worn-out or lost guns in Ethiopia and Spain.

▲ Italian artillerymen in the Libyan desert with a 65/17 shielded cannon.

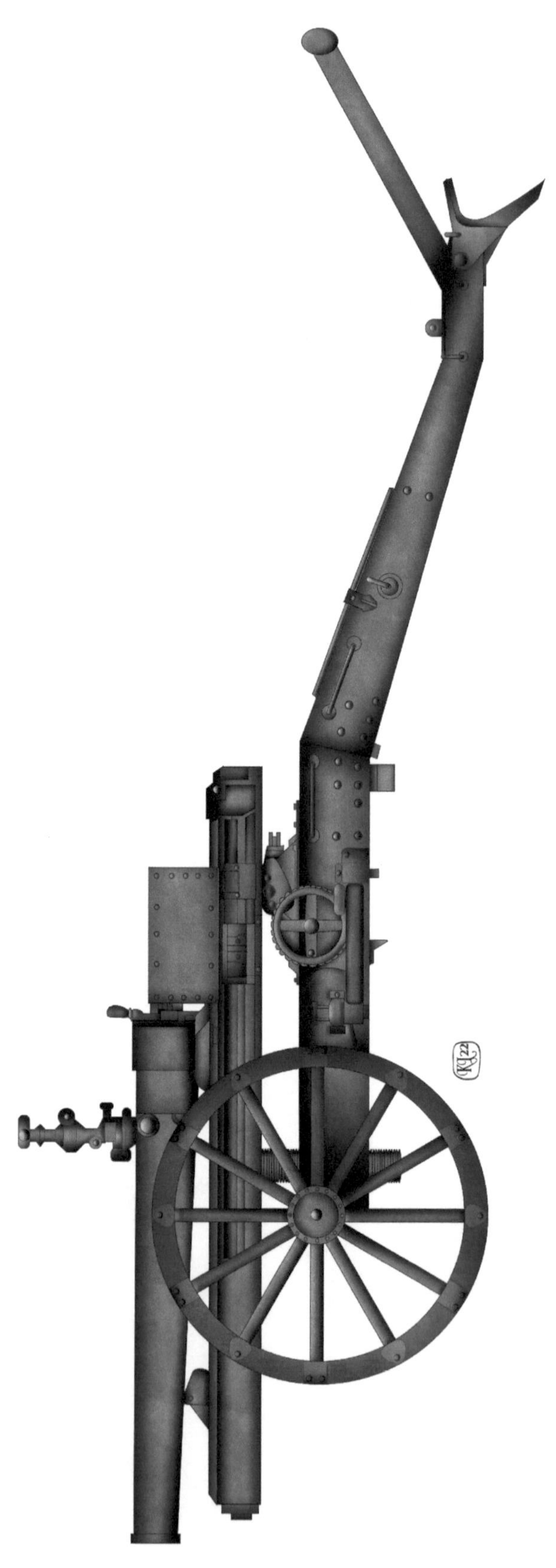

Despite its early retirement, the old 65/17 was still widely used on all fronts during the war. In fact, it was noted that, in spite of its old design, the gun soon proved to be superior to the 47/32 which had been created precisely to replace the 65/17 in the anti-tank role, especially thanks to the powerful armour-piercing and EP projectiles that were distributed from 1942 onwards. In the Libyan deserts, the old piece experienced a second life, soon becoming the weapon of choice due to its inherent versatility.

The Libyan workshops of the 12th AS Auto Raggruppamento made several lorry mounted guns based on the chassis of pre-war Fiat 634 and Morris CS8 trucks, creating 'flying batteries' known as "batterie volanti" to try to counter the increased power of the British armoured forces. During the Tunisian campaign, the 80th Artillery Regiment of the 'La Spezia' (80th) self-transporter division was rearmed entirely on 65/17s, towed by Moto Guzzi Trialce motor trucks (see photo on page 13). In Italian East Africa, the piece, designed to be broken down, ended up equipping Colonial camel batteries. It was also widely used in Dalmatia where it was even used to arm anti-landing coastal batteries. RSI units and even the Germans after the armistice also put it into service, christening it the 6.5 cm GebK-246(i).

▲ East Africa 1935. Black shirts of the "28th October" carry two 65/17 cannons with wooden wheels.(Author's collection).

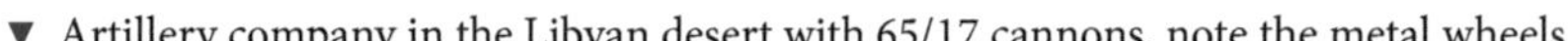

▼ Artillery company in the Libyan desert with 65/17 cannons, note the metal wheels.

The barrel was steel with left-hand rifling; the screw-type breech block was quick-action, equipped with semi-automatic case ejection and recocking; the barrel was fixed on a sleigh that slides on the carriage, containing a hydraulic recuperator with a spring to return, the cradle was mounted on a single-tailed take downable carriage with rigid axle, and wooden later Elektron, 700 mm diameter wheels. The use of a movable and foldable gun shield in order to gave crew protection. In the numerous pictures available, however, it is clear that it was used sporadically. Aiming in the direction (8°) was achieved by swinging the cradle carrier on the semi-circular rails of the shaft, while elevation was achieved by rotating the cradle on the trunnions, set far back. Curious note: the 65/17 was the first Italian gun equipped with safety devices against accidental opening of the breech to limit premature and accidental firing and to protect against ignition delays in the ammunition.

The light artillery version was transportable by mules by breaking it down into five parts, already indicated. The version assigned to infantry sections was also towable by means of a metal cradle, which could also be transported by mules. Commissioning for movement was particularly fast and took only a few minutes.

Ordinary ammunition consisted of a 'wrapped shell', but in addition to this standard there were also other projectiles: **shrapnel round**, with graduated fuse mod. 912, usually coloured blue with an orange stripe. A **training round**, without explosive and internal mechanisms, coloured light green. A **blank round**, with reduced charge and softwood projectile to allow the semi automatic breech block to function. Double-action shell (abolished by order of 1 August 1935). **Armour-piercing round**, with fuse I-90-909-R.M. The ammunition was transported in special boxes with handles (for hand carriage). Each chest contained 10 cases and two primer boxes of 12 pieces each. Each mule could carry two loads , each weighing about 66 kg.

▲ Guadalajara, Italian Volunteer Corps artillerymen in Spain with a 65/17.

▲ Auto-cannon with 65/17 next to one with Breda anti-aircraft, mounted on a Morris truck.

▼ 65-17 model 1913 cannon in a military museum. Wikipedia photo by Fat yankey.

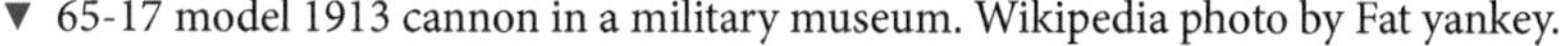

OBICE 75/13

Skoda 7.5 cm Vz. 1915 or 7.5 cm Gebirgskanone M. 15: this was the first name of this good weapon, an Austrian mountain howitzer used during the Great War. It was so well conceived that even the Germans, second to none in the art of gun production, adopted the small Gebirgskanone.

Italy got its first specimens in a somewhat adventurous way, by seizing an Austrian steamer at sea in 1915 during neutrality with some Skoda 7.5s on board destined for export to China. The ship was interned in Naples with its cargo, but upon entry into the war on 24 May, the cargo was finally requisitioned by the army. Having ascertained the good quality of the piece, a batch of parts was entrusted to Ansaldo. When the war was over and won, Italy also obtained, by way of reparations, several guns from the former enemy; to be precise, a total of almost 700 were added to the Royal Arsenal. These were immediately distributed among the (destined units, i.e the) Alpine and mountain units (in this respect, the 75/13 proved to be more powerful than the small Italian 65/17).

Indeed, it had considerable ballistic advantages, a greater firing angle and the possibility of firing a greater variety of projectiles. On the other hand, having a need 'to be carried', its weight was greater and required at least a couple of extra mules for transport. Nevertheless, the gun was much appreciated, and the Italian arsenals continued its production. Between production and orders, by 1941 the army had 1450 pieces, many of which were located in the Alpine defensive positions facing France. The 75/13 had its baptism of fire in Abyssinia and then in the Spanish Civil War. In East Africa, some 300 pieces were issued to Italian forces.

The fact remains that, for all its merits, by the 1930s it had begun to show its age, especially when compared to more modern contemporaries. However, given the nation's poor economic situation, the idea of replacing the gun with a more modern and high-performance one, was planned but stymied, and at the end of 1942 there were still over 1,200 pieces in service.

▲ An Austrian Škoda 7.5 cm Gebirgskanone M.15. Symbol of the Alpine war in 1915-18.

75/13 HOWITZER AUSTRO-HUNGARIAN WAR PREY - EUROPEAN THEATRE 1940-1945

The gun operated on all war fronts except North Africa. It was mainly used on the Greek-Albanian front, which was particularly suited to its characteristics. There, in the early part of 1941, over 600 were sent. A much smaller number were also sent to Russia and a few dozen to the AOI (Italian Eastern Africa). In the Russian steppes, it was used in the anti tank role by the Alpine divisions.

After the armistice, the piece was 'inherited' by the RSI and the CIL. The Germans, however, also participated in the division, and the Wehrmacht, together with the 29. Waffen-Grenadier Division der SS, used it extensively under the designation of *7.5 cm GebK 259(i)* (Italian mountain gun 259 75 mm).

After the war, the obsolescent 75/13 was assigned to the reconstituted Italian Army, which put it back into service in the mountain batteries of the Alpine brigades (*Taurinense*, *Tridentina*, *Julia* and later *Orobica* and *Cadore*), until it was finally replaced by the 105/14 Mod 56 in the late 1960s.

Thus, what had been the Skoda, the 7.5 cm Gebirgeschutze M. 15, probably the best mountain gun, was put into the line by our adversaries shortly after the outbreak of the Great War, would end up being retired almost half a century later.

Today, this cannon, along with others, can frequently be encountered in the courtyards of Alpine barracks, in town squares, in remembrance parks all over Italy, often used by animated children who almost certainly have no idea what stories these weapons hide.

SPECIFICATIONS:	
Entry into service	1920
Weight in battery	620 kg
Projectile weight	5 kg
Initial projectile speed	354 m/sec
Horizontal firing sector	7°
Vertical firing sector	-10° / +50°
Maximum range	8.200 metri
Rate of fire	min 6/max 10 al minuto
Number of pieces available in 1942	1213

▲ An Italian 75/13 ex Austrian Škoda 7.5 cm. Preserved in the park of the Rocca di Bergamo. Photo by the author.

■ SPECIFICATIONS

The 75/13 cannon was intended to be moved by animals as pack gun, and could be divided into seven parts ,loaded on as many mules; the heaviest load was 106 kg and the minimum load 100 kg (trail and wheels); the weight of the mules' pack and harness added about another 45 kg to the load of the animal so one can imagine the fatigue of the animal and also that of the Alpine soldiers. There are countless photos showing soldiers carrying components, when it was was broken down into the following 7 loads: howitzer barrel - breech block - sleigh - carriage - trail and wheels - gun shields.

The battery ammunition was transported by pack mule. Each mule carried four boxes, each of which contained three rounds. These boxes carried the rounds with the head kept separated from the cartridge case by a crossbar. The piece could also be towed on roads with not too steep an incline, due to the lack of a brake.

The barrel was made of steel, consisting of a tube, sleeve for attaching the breech block.

The breechwas a horizontal wedge type, with firing controls on the right enabling rapid target acquisition with the firing, and recocking levers. Finally, the muzzle was single-tailed, moving on the carriage for aiming; recoil-retracted and variable recoil; recoil mass increase with sleeve slide. Firing brake with rotating sleeve; spring-loaded recoil pad.

Ordinary 75/13 ammunition in 1943 consisted of:

- 75 shell containing 370 g TNT, at 354 m/s
- large capacity shell containing 670 g TNT, at 378 m/s
- 75/13 mod 32 grenade (610 g TNT, vo 349 m/s)[8]
- 75 shrapnel (216 pallets Ø 12.7 mm and 13.4 mm, vo 356 m/s)[9]
- 75 mod 32 rear-piercing grenade (270 g explosive, vo 350 m/s)[10]
- EP grenade (hollow charge)
- EPS grenade mod 42 (vo 396 m/s)[11]
- gas grenade (tear gas, vesicant, irritant)
- smoke grenade
- large-capacity grenade loaded with white phosphorus
- grenade for training (smoke shell)

▲ A 75/13 towed by Alpine troops in battery.

▲ A 75/17 towed by a single mule.

▲ Details of the 75/13 preserved in the park of the Rocca di Bergamo. Photo by the author.

75/27 CANNON - SPANISH THEATRE 1936-1939 AND EUROPEAN THEATRE 1940-1945

CANNON 75/27

This name refers to three different models: the 1906, 1911 and 1912. As the name of the first model implies, it all began in 1906 when the Royal Army brought the 75 mm Krupp rapid-fire gun into service, which had its baptism of fire in 1910 during the Libyan War.

However, the operational evaluation of the gun's performance was not the best. The weapon was blamed for a lack of mobility in varied terrain and an excessively small arc of fire. In light of these problems, the choice of Krupp was reconsidered. Three different suppliers were now competing: Schneider, Déport and Krupp. Following trials, it was decided to go with the Déport 75 mm rapid-fire model. The actual production of the gun took place under licence by a consortium of several companies headed by Vickers-Terni and Società Acciaierie Terni.

The 75/27 Mod. 1911 then joined the Mod. 1906 in the campaign artillery regiments. The approaching First World War urgently required a good number of these guns, but Krupp could no longer supply its guns directly, which were from then on commissioned directly from Ansaldo.

At the outbreak of war in 1915, Italy had 500 of both models of the 75/27 in service. All these guns were issued to the artillery regiments of the infantry divisions and army corps. The *75/27 Mod. 1911,* thanks to its superior characteristics compared to the corresponding Austrian material (Škoda *8 cm Vz. 1905*), allowed the Italian field artillery to operate advantageously against the enemy.

In the course of the war, the number of guns of both models grew dramatically, so that by November 1917, 488 batteries with 1931 guns of both models were in service. The defeat at Caporetto resulted in the loss of about 200 of these guns, nevertheless, at the end of the conflict, around 800 of the 75/27 mod. 11 were still in sevice.

Because of its flexible design, the 75/27 Mod. 11 was also soon used in anti-aircraft defence, which was possible at the time due to the low speed of aircraft, and it was the piece most widely used by the Regio Esercito in anti-aircraft duties during the conflict, eventually arming 43 batteries towards the end of the war. The Mod. 11 was recognised as a good weapon, attracting the interest of France, Russia and Romania, who ordered a number of guns.

▲ A 75/27 mod. 11 preserved at the Vittoriale degli italiani in Gardone (BS). Photo by the author.

75/27 CANNON - NORTH AFRICAN THEATRE 1940-1945

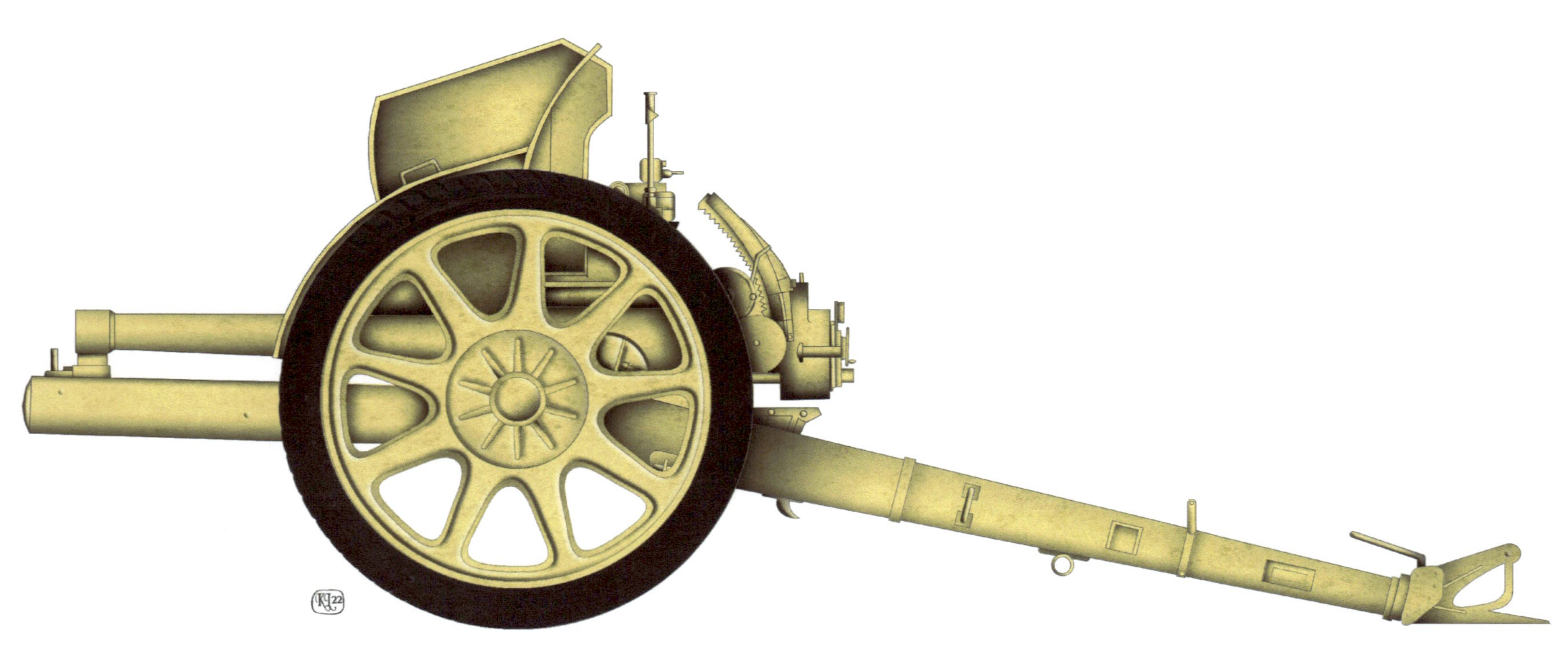

	Mod. 1906	Mod. 1911*
Entry into service	1906	1911
Weight in battery	1.015 kg	1.075 kg
Bullet weight	6,3 kg	6,3 kg
Total muzzle length	2,250 metres	2,132 metres
Firing angle	7°	53°
Vertical field of fire	-10° / +16°	-15° / +65°
Maximum range	10.200 metres	10.200
Rate of fire	min 6/max 8 per minute	min 6/max 8 per minute
Number of pieces available June 1940	1699	1341

* The third model, 75/17 Mod. 1912, was a development of the Mod. 1906, designed for use as horse artillery. At the outbreak of the Second World War, only about 50 were made available and assigned to the artillery regiments of the Rapid Divisions, operating mainly in Russia. When the CSIR was later taken over by the ARMIR, this piece was decommissioned and replaced with the Model 1911.

After the First World War, the piece remained with the artillery regiments of the infantry divisions. Improvements and refinements were made to the piece, in particular to achieve a longer range of at least 12 km and to adapt the piece to mechanised towing. The range problem was solved by working on new cartridge case ammunition, i.e. a variable charge, which increased the range by 2 km.

The adaptation to the self-propelled elastic carriage, on which the gun was loaded, entailed the overhaul of the wooden wheels, which were largely replaced by rubberised metal wheels, at least for the units assigned to the motorised units. However, during the Second World War, numerous 75/27 guns with the original wooden wheels were routinely encountered (the same applied to larger calibre units, such as the 105/28 and 105/32).

However, the long and unusual shape of the cannon caused quite a few difficulties for the towing system adopted. The problem would only be solved some time later with the use of Pavesi P4 wheeled tractors,

▲ Battery of 75/27s towed by Fiat-SPA TL37. Note the elastic undercarriage. Wikipedia cc1 licence.

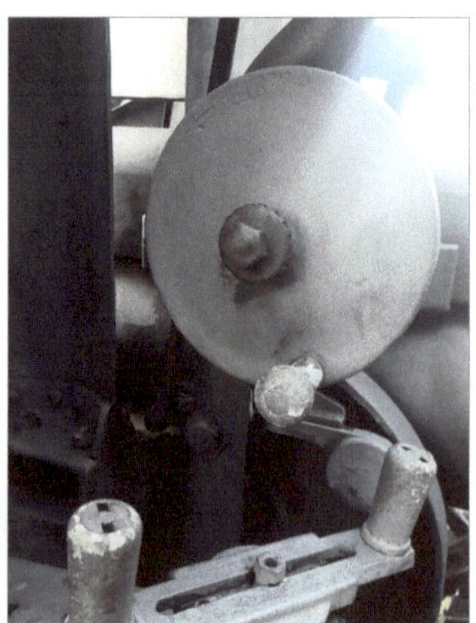

▲ Details of the 75/27 preserved in the park of the Rocca di Bergamo. Photo by the author.

and later Fiat-OCI 708 CM tracked and TL37 wheeled tractors. In 1936, about a hundred of these were sent to Spain to participate with the CTV in the Spanish Civil War.

As already mentioned for all the low calibres, the 75/27 was completely obsolete for use as artillery, due to the poor effectiveness of the shells.

In 1940, Italy, along with France,were the only countries that still had artillery of this calibre first line service, while the other nations kept these pieces in reserve.

The *75/27 Mod. 1911* cannons were sold to Poland and given to Spain after the Civil War. It is esti-mated that around 330 were sold.

■ THE SECOND WORLD WAR

At the outbreak of the conflict, most of the artillery was still horse-drawn, and as far as the *75/27 Mod. 11s were concerned*, only 268 of the 1,300 available were prepared for mechanical towing.

Like other weapons, not all fronts saw the presence of this weapon, and specifically the *75/27 Mod. 11* gun was not made operational in East Africa.

The *75/27 Mod. 1911s* were used heavily on the Russian front, while on the North African front both models were used, but the more basic *75/27 Mod. 1906* was preferred. There were 138 pieces in Libya in 1942, reduced to 10 after the Battle of El Alamein and the abandonment of Africa.

This gun, like the other light calibres, ended up filling the anti tank role, also using hollow charge shells; however, analyses and studies made by German engineers on the real effectiveness of the 75/27's an-ti-tank use was completely disarming. Shooting against Soviet T-34 tanks only 'tickled' them. In spite of this, the General Staff continued to use it (even in this key), only to find, beyond reasonable doubt, that it was only effective when fired at distances of 100 metres.. After 8 September 1943, as was the custom for every Italian weapon available, the 75/27 pieces were also requisitioned by the Germans and renamed **7.5 cm FK 244(i)** by them.

▲ A 75/27 mod.11 next to its front end. Preserved in the park of the Rocca di Bergamo. Photo by the author.

The piece was on a rotating shaft, based on wooden spoked wheels, which were obsolete in the Second World War as they severely limited the possibility of mechanical towing. This in summary was the most serious problem, along with the low calibre. The barrel was made up of two pieces, a core and a sleeve, connected to the cradle by two recuperators for guidance during recoil. The breech block was screw-type, with a seal ensured by the expansion of the brass case. The firing mechanism was attached to the block, and consisted of a hammer, firing pin, trigger, cocking lever.

The first 1906 model was immediately recognisable by the shape of the tail, which was single, while it was of the double-tailed type for the Mod. 1911. This greatly improved the stability of the operational piece by allowing four points of support on the ground.

The recoil system was combined to allow the piece to recoil at high elevation without the risk of the breech hitting the ground during recoil. The combined recoil system was achieved by equipping the gun with two independent springs, not present on the 1906 model.

The elevation device acted on the cradle of the barrel, so elevation could be achieved by acting on both the carriage and the gun mount.

The tails of the Model 1911 were made of sheet metal with a rectangular cross-section and terminated with a swivel in which spades were fixed. Attached to the gun were the 4 mm thick shield and the brake for manual locking of the wheels. The aiming mechanism was a panoramic telescope equipped with correction devices for correcting shot fall.

Animal towing required three pairs, for a total of six horses and was carried out by attaching to the gun, a limber containing 32 shells, on which up to three crew could be placed. For mechanical towing typically with a Fiat-SPA TL37 artillery tractor, the piece was loaded onto a spring-loaded bogie placed inside its wheels, under the carriage.

Typical 75/27 ammunition in the First World War

- grenade loaded with TNT or schneiderite
- shrapnel loaded with 360 9 g or 260 12 g pellets
- Schneider percussion fuse grenade (French construction)
- disruptive grenade for anti-aircraft fire
- chemical grenade with 400 g of tear gas or asphyxiant gas or fog mixture
- inert grenade (for drill)

Typical 75/27 ammunition in the Second World War

- ordinary 75 grenade
- pallet-loaded shrapnel
- large-capacity grenade
- miter box (238 16 mm lead pellets)
- exploding armour-piercing grenade
- grenade Mod. 32
- ordinary grenade Mod. 34/36
- double-acting grenade
- grenade 1900/15N (of French origin)
- grenade Mod. 17 (of French origin)
- EP grenades (ready effect) or EPS (special ready effect) or EPS Mod. 42 (hollow charge)
- high-capacity smoke/incendiary projectiles
- tear gas or vesicant chemical grenade
- special loading grenade for training

▲ Details of the 75/27 and its front end preserved at the Rocca park in Bergamo. Photo by the author.

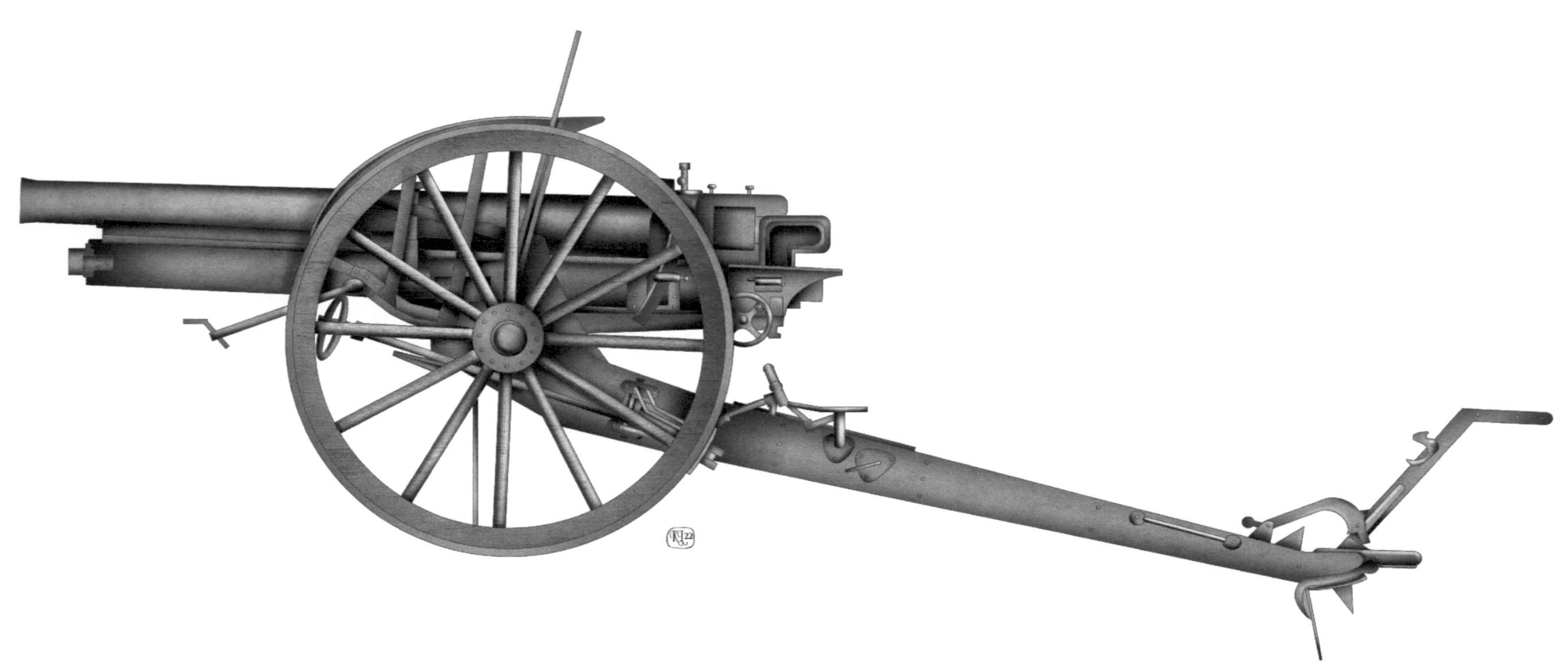

77/28 CANNON

Another gun of wartime provenance, the 77/28 was none other than the Austro-Hungarian Böhler 8 cm Vz. 1905 or 8 cm Feldkanone M.5., born and conceived as a field gun. In this capacity it was employed by the Austro-Hungarian Imperial Royal Army and, from the first post-war period, by several other nations. Italy acquired a fair number of them both as *spoils of war and on account of war reparations, and used them in its units like many other Austro-Hungarian weapons. Built by Böhler, after the war, all subsequent variants such as the Mod. 5/8 were developed by Skoda.

The approximately 250 77/28 guns that Italy brought at the outbreak of World War II were conceived from their birth for use in the mountains, so they could be disassembled and packed into three separate loads.

The Regio Esercito used the Austrian gun mainly in its own colonies, considering it to be an outdated model and therefore only used as a position and defence piece. In AOI (where Italy wanted to save on war material) it constituted the bulk of the artillery deployed in that campaign. As with all the colonies, the 77/28 was also present in Libya in the frontier areas, and therefore almost all were lost during the first British offensive in 1940.

The remaining 77/28s from 1942 onwards were redistributed to the 'Brescia', 'Bologna' and 'Pavia' divisions in North Africa in an anti-tank role. These divisions took part in the El Alamein campaign and subsequent retreat to Tunisia. Here, the few remaining pieces were assigned to divisions, such as the "Centauro", "Spezia" and "Trieste", as well as to the Saharan Regiment.

After September 1943, some of these guns were captured by (Nazi) Germany, changing their designation to 7.65 cm FK(i) (i= italien). The original version ceased service altogether after World War II, with only a few remaining in arsenals in Italy.

▲ The Austro-Hungarian Böhler 8 cm cannon Vz. 1905 or 8 cm Feldkanone M. 5, (77/28 in Italy). Wikipedia.

Of conventional design, its main feature and one that immediately stood out was the obsolete and anachronistic bronze barrel. It was the result of a forced situation as the Austro-Hungarian Empire had had serious difficulties in producing steel of adequate quality.

This fact, along with others, led to slow progress in the design and creation of the cannon. The main problem was caused by indecision over the recoil system and type of breech. This barrel, either plain or tubular steel, weighed around 355 kg together with the fast-moving horizontal wedge breech block; with its dovetail slide, it fitted onto the cradle, which housed the hydropneumatic recoil reducer with grooves in the cylinder with the recoil spring for return to battery. The carriage was single-tailed, with 1300 mm diameter wooden wheels and a 1610 mm track on the 4.5 mm thick shield.

On the outer shield were two seats for the assistants in a position on either side of the barrel. The towing was by 3 pairs of horses and was done by hitching the piece to a forecarriage, thus composed it reached a weight of 1900 kg.

In addition to the obsolescent animal towing, the 77/28 was later adapted to mechanical towing with the elastic undercarriage system. In other cases, the Royal Army also adopted it for road transport, loading the piece by attaching it to the body of a truck.

Mod. 5/8

The Mod. 5/8 differed from the others in that, for towing in the mountains, it could be broken down and transported (towed) in three sections on special trolleys. This consisted of:
- *gun and mount* weighing 685 kg;
- *shield and tail* weighing 500 kg;
- 500 kg *heavy car.*

Typical 77/28 ammunition during World War II:

- original 77 d.e. grenade: steel, heavy (complete grenade shell) 6.400 kg, loaded with molten TNT or toluolammonal or 60/40 explosive.

- original 77 ring grenade: steel, heavy (complete shell casing) 6.530 kg, loaded with toluolammonal or ecrasite or 60/40 explosive.

- original 77 grenade: steel, heavy (complete grenade shell) 4.800 kg, loaded with ammonal.

- 77 grenade: steel, heavy (complete shell casing) 6.240 kg, loaded with molten TNT or toluolammonal or 60/40 explosive.

- 77 short grenade: steel, heavy (full grenade shell) 4.695 or 4.687 kg, loaded with TNT or ammonal.

- 77 grenade-shrapnel: steel, with lead pellets, weighing (complete grenade shell) 6.50 kg.

- 77 grenade-shrapnel: steel, with iron pallets, weighing (complete grenade shell) 6.50 kg.

- original 77 grenade: steel, with lead pellets, weighing (complete grenade shell) 6.64 kg.

- original 77 grenade: steel, with iron pallets, weighing (complete grenade shell) 5.65 kg.

- 77 shrapnel: steel, with lead and iron pallets, weighing (complete shell casing) 5.619 kg.

- 77/28 miter box: the miter box is a zinc casing containing 210 lead-antimony pellets.

SPECIFICATIONS:	
Entry into service	1917
Weight in battery	1.050 kg
Projectile weight	6,4 kg
Initial projectile speed	554 m/sec
Firing angle	8°
Vertical field of fire	-7° / +18°
Maximum range	7.300 metres
Rate of fire	10 per minute
Number of pieces available in 1940	245

▲ Two more images of the Austro-Hungarian Böhler 8 cm cannon Vz. 1905. Wikipedia.

▲ A 77/28 preserved at the Parco delle Rimembranze in Merate (LC). Small (above) a 77/28 of the Italian army in North Africa circa 1942. Smaller (below) a 77/28 fitted with tyred wheels. Rovereto War History Museum. Finazzer Archive.

▲ Various details of the 77/28 preserved in theme parks. Wikipedia CC1.

OBICE 100/17

As already extensively mentioned, at the end of the First World War, Italy had acquired a huge amount of war material from the now former Austro-Hungarian enemy as war reparations. For the army, the main bulk consisted of artillery. This also included the 100/17 howitzer, also made by Skoda before the war, which was later produced in two models, one in 1914 and the next in 1916 as a mountain gun. In the Italian arsenals in the early 1920s, there were no less than 2694 100/17 howitzers, of which 1222 were acquired as war supplies, the remainder as war reparations.

During the First World War and throughout the conflict, the piece demonstrated excellent overall performance. The 100/17 was a simple howitzer, very robust and compact, capable of firing and operating for a long time without any problems. The pieces, once acquired by Italy, were all overhauled by the Arsenal del Regio Esercito di Torino (ARET), which also worked with third parties. Among the most significant improvements in 1932 was the adoption of new projectiles, the Mod. 32, which enabled a longer range of about 500 m.

The 100/17 had its baptism of fire in AOI and was later used by the Volunteer Troops Corps in the Spanish Civil War. Part of these pieces was later given to Spain. In 1919, Škoda, by then no longer an Austrian company, produced for the Czechoslovak army a version of the field gun with an elongated barrel with 24 calibres (22 according to the Italian system) called the Škoda 10 cm Vz. 1914/1919, which was adopted by Poland, Greece and Yugoslavia. These were captured and redeployed by the Wehrmacht, who gave some of them to the Regio Esercito during the war, which were renamed 105/22. The most famous of these pieces still fires a blank shot from the Janiculum every day to remind all Romans of noon.

The pieces equipped many of the Frontier Guard's position batteries, while the Royal Army assigned one battery to each divisional artillery regiment. At the beginning of the Second War, the Royal Army had: 325 *Mod. 14 howitzers* towed by animals or in fixed positions, 199 *Mod. 14* howitzers mechanically towed and 181 *Mod. 16* mountain howitzers. In operations, especially in the Libyan desert, the 100/17s soon proved to be inferior to their opponent's counterpart, the British 25-pounder.

As with many other ex-WW1 guns, the 'autarkic' meaning self reliant and ingenious Libyan workshops installed the piece on the Lancia 3Ro truck, resulting in the 100/17 truck. In June 1943, there were still 37 *Mod. 14* howitzer gun units available for the Regio Esercito.

▲ 100/17 Skoda howitzer overhauled Italy. Parco della Rocca di Bergamo (photo by the author).

100/17 HOWITZER MOD. 14 - EUROPEAN AND NATIONAL THEATRE 1940-1945

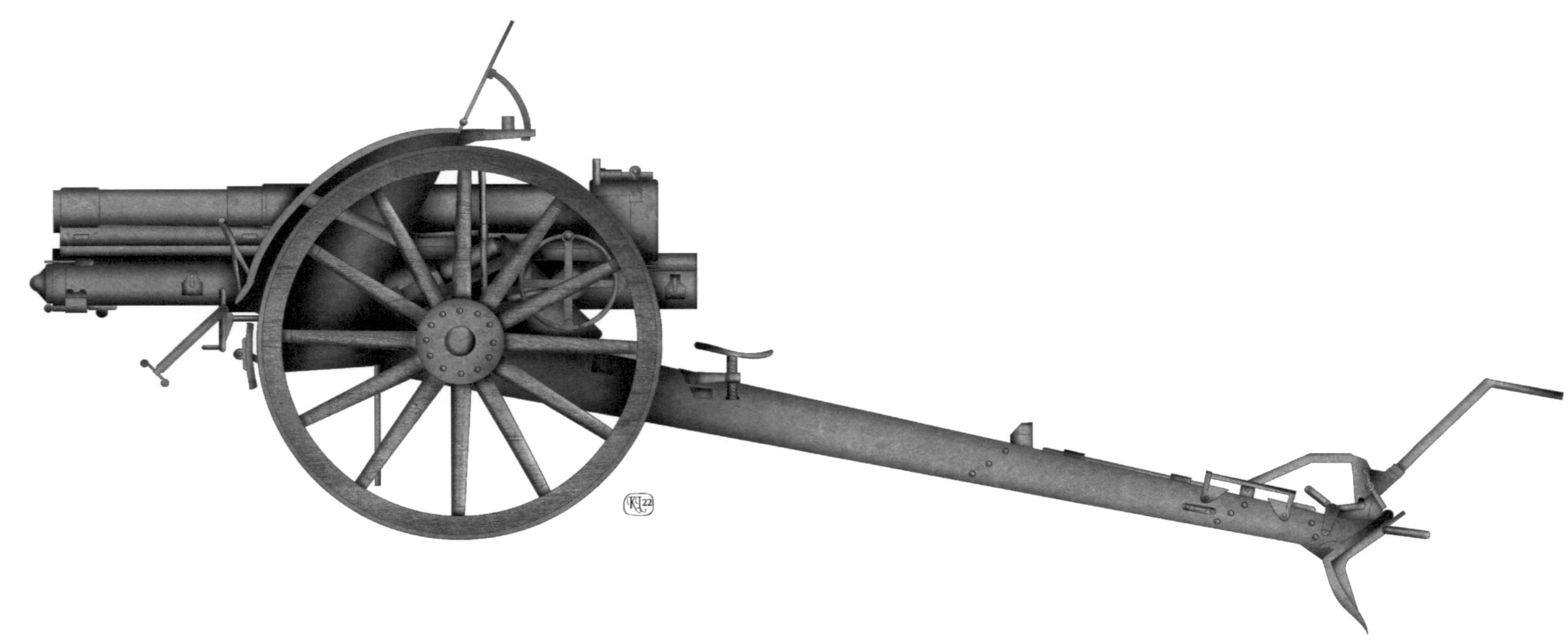

SPECIFICATIONS:	
Entry into service	1914
Weight in battery	1.417 kg
Projectile weight	11,50 / 13,8 kg
Initial projectile speed	430 m/sec
Firing angle	5°
Vertical field of fire	-8° / +48°
Maximum range	9.200 metres
Rate of fire	4/6 colpi per minute
Number of pieces available in 1940	1.705

Even the 100/17, although very unsuitable for the purpose, was sometimes used in an anti-tank role, with hollow charge projectiles EP, available from the second half of 1942 and EPS available from May 1943, which were also effective against Soviet T-34s, were made available for this role.

In addition to the specimens captured by the Germans after 8 September 1943 (renamed *10 cm leFH 315(i)*), some pieces were, as was customary, used by units of the RSI.

Later, after the Second World War, the piece was adapted for use as mountain artillery, with the designations '100/17 Mod. 14 mont' and '100/17 Mod. 16 mont' after a series of modifications at the Naples Military Arsenal. The piece remained operational for about another 40 years!

▲ Details of the 100/17 Skoda howitzer overhauled in Italy. Parco della Rocca di Bergamo (photo by the author).

▲ Details of howitzer 100/17 mod. 32. At the Pontida (BG) shrine. Photo by the author.

■ SPECIFICATIONS

The howitzer was well made of steel and had a wedge-shaped breech block with a horizontal opening and was thus easy to use even for recruits; the gun was single-tailed but with a wide central opening that favoured a high elevation. As it was a fairly heavy piece, unlike the smaller 65 and partly 75 calibre, it always had to be towed (in the Austro-Hungarian army, towing was by animal only). But by the 1930s and 1940s, the time was ripe to move to operational mechanisation. The Regio Esercito therefore wanted to equip it with the Fiat-SPA TL37 artillery tractor but to make it possible; the old wooden wheels had to be replaced, as we have seen in all the models mentioned so far. The old wheels therefore had to be replaced with Elektron models suitable for road travel by installing the usual elastic undercarriage. The piece thus modernised received the Italian designation of 100/17 mod. 35, which then joined the remaining mod. 14 and mod. 16. These, together with the 75/27, formed the great backbone of the Italian divisional artillery. As proof of the howitzer's good workmanship, it suffices to mention that it remained operational in the Italian army until the early 1980s!

Typical 77/28 ammunition during World War II:
- 100 explosive grenade
- 100-round grenade
- shrapnel grenade 100
- 100 grenade Mod. 32
- 100 Mod. 32 double-acting grenade
- 100 Mod. 36 double-acting grenade
- EP perforating projector (ready effect - hollow charge)
- EPS perforating projector (special ready effect - hollow charge)
- grenade Mod. 23 (Polish)
- grenade Mod. 28 (Polish)
- 100 Mod. 32 grenade with blistering tang
- 100 Mod. 32 tear-gas grenade
- 100 Mod. 32 smoke grenade
- 100 Mod. 32 smoke grenade
- 100 Mod. 32 grenade with irritant container

▲ Details of howitzer 100/17 Mod. 32. Parco della Rocca di Bergamo (photo by the author).

CANNON 105/28

The 105/28 gun was an artillery piece intended for and then used by the Royal Army during the First and Second World Wars as field heavy artillery a term that mutated into army corps artillery from 1935 to 1946. The 105/28 was present virtually everywhere besides Italy, on the North African front, the Greek front and also on the Russian front.

Before World War 1, like other pieces, it was used to equip some of the Italian Army's heavy field artillery batteries. The main reason for the adoption of the piece, as mentioned, was to replace the old 75s and to be used alongside the 149/12 howitzers. The General Staff then opted for the French Schneider model itself derived from the Russian 107mm Putilov, the production of which was licensed to Ansaldo.

At the time, it came close to a diplomatic incident, as Italy was still an ally of Germany at the time. The gun was then secretly ordered from Ansaldo (linked to Schneider) in July 1914, requiring only minor modifications, the most notable of which concerned the aiming of the piece.

Production of the 105/28 began in September 1914, and it was operational in September 1916. It was flanked by 149-A howitzers in the field heavy artillery groups, assigned at army corps level. The tasks of this gun duo were counter-battery fire, fire against enemy troops and action against troops in cover and against fortifications and entrenchments.

Shortly before the end of the war, 426 guns were on the line in 1918. Compared to the corresponding Austrian guns, the 105/28 had a shorter range of about 2 km, but, weighing much less, was more manoeuvrable. Another great advantage of the 105/28 was the safety of the piece, which recorded very few technical problems and accidents throughout the conflict.

After the First World War, and especially in the 1930s, the General Staff felt the need to adapt these pieces for mechanical towing as well. The traditional solution was the usual elastic undercarriage with suspension, which was used for towing. The tractor initially chosen was the heavy truck Fiat 18 BLR and other tractors, later replaced by the reliable Pavesi P4. In addition to the gun, mechanical towing was also used for the ammunition, with a special trailer (Arato-type tow truck mod.34) carrying 100 to 120 complete rounds for the piece. A defect that was immediately found was the low speed of the Pavesi of only around 18 km/h, while elsewhere they already claimed an average towing speed of around 40 km/h. To remedy this, the piece's wooden wheels were finally replaced in 1937, using stronger Elektron wheels.

▲ The 105/28 cannon (Schneider). Wikipedia CC1.

During the Second World War, considering the shortage of materials, the wheels were made of sheet steel. During the same years, similar guns from other nations could boast much longer ranges and, as the main purpose of these pieces was counter-battery fire, the 105/28 also had to be upgraded. The ammunition was therefore modified by increasing the range to 12780 m with the new Mod 32 and Mod 32G shells; however, these resulted in significant barrel wear, which presented new problems for the piece.

During the course of the Abyssinian War, the 105/28 was only present in a very few batteries, which then grew with the outbreak of the Second World War, bringing the piece in AOI to around sixty guns. In the Spanish Civil War, however, as many as 403 105/28 guns were used. In 1940, there were eight 105/28 groups in Cyrenaica, in all about 100 guns. Most of these were immediately lost in the first devastating British offensive. Subsequently, the African pieces were replaced and participated in the subsequent operations up to El Alamein and the subsequent retreat to Tunisia. None of these returned to Italy.

At the beginning of the Greek campaign in October 1940, three groups were deployed. During the Russian campaign, at the time of the change between CSIR and ARMIR, the Regio Esercito decided to equip its units with good numbers of the 105/28. Again, as in Africa, all the guns were lost as a result of the Soviet offensive in the winter of 1942, which led to the destruction of the ARMIR.

Following the armistice of 1943, several dozen were immediately requisitioned by the Germans, who named them *10.5 cm Kan 338(i)*. Some later passed into the hands of RSI units. While the Southern Kingdom forces who fought with the allies equipped a group of 105/28s in the *First Motorised Regiment* and later the *Italian Liberation Corps*. The piece was decommissioned in 1951.

▲ Left: 105/28 cannon belonging to the CIL fires at German units. Right: Italian artillerymen in Cyrenaica with a 105/28. Wikipedia CC1.

■ SPECIFICATIONS

The 105/28 gun rested on a gun mount supported with large-diameter, iron-rimmed wooden spoke wheels and gun shield. The original characteristic of the mount was its ability to move on the gun carriage for an arc of about 14°. The barrel was just under three metres long, made of steel and was equipped with a 4-sector breech block. The barrel was reinforced at the rear by a sleeve, which was attached to the body. This sleeve extended from the breech to half the length of the barrel, with reinforcement at the rear, which served to hold the trunnions in a barycentric position, thus avoiding the need for balancers. The sighting device was on a drum elevation, with a Cortese-Falcone model panoramic scope.
Originally, the piece was animal-drawn, with parades of horses.

Typical 105/28 ammunition during World War II:

- 105 one-piece grenade (15.5 kg, V0 565 m/s, range 11425 m) consumable
- 105 steel cast iron grenade (15.4 kg, V0 445 m/s, range 10980 m) at consumption
- 105 mod 32 grenade (16.3 kg, V0 576 m/s, range 12780 m)
- 105 mod 32G grenade (16.15 kg, V0 576, range 12780 m)
- 105 mod 32 double-acting grenade (15.125 kg, V0 570 m/s, range 13640 m) consumable
- 105 mod 36 double-acting grenade (16.2 kg, V0 570 m/s, range 13640 m)
- 105 mod 36 G double-acting grenade (15.9 kg, V0 579 m/s)
- 105 armour-piercing grenade (15.65 kg, V0 579, range 2500 m)
- 105/28-32 (16.65 kg) armour-piercing grenade in experimental phase
- 105 (16.65 kg) semi-perforating grenade in experimental phase
- 105-round grenade mod 43 EP (14 kg, V0 602 m/s, range 12360 m) hollow-charged
- 105 grenade mod 43 (14 kg, V0 510 m/s, range 9400 m)
- 105 smoke grenade
- 105 smoke grenade
- 105 inert grenade (for drill)

▲ Details of the 105/28 cannon. Various Italian war parks and museums. Wikipedia and others.

FIAT 20-B TRACTOR

Dating back to 1915, it was the first tractor produced by Fiat, officially called the Type 20 heavy tractor. It was equipped with a Fiat 67 A engine with a power output of 60HP, 4-stroke petrol engine.
It was one of the Regio Esercito's first artillery tractors along with the Pavesi Tolotti A and B. We have included it as the first and most archaic of the machines designed for towing cannons and howitzers. It took part in the entire First World War, remaining in operation even after the war until the 1930s when it was replaced by more modern tractors. It was later replaced by the Breda 32 heavy tractor, which ended the fleet of tractors adopted during the Great War and which had basically remained in service up to that time, namely the Fiat type 20, the Pavesi-Tolotti type B, the FIAT 18BLR, and also the Austrian Daimler war tractor.

SPECIFICATIONS:	
Entry into service	1914
Full load weight	11.500 kg
Chassis length	5,5 metres
Wheelbase	3,5 metres
Vehicle height	2,9 metres
Vehicle width	2,3 metres
Maximum speed	12 km/h
Tank capacity	240 litres
Number of parts available in 1940	N.A.

▲ In the large photo Fiat 20 b tractors with tracks engaged in towing big cannons 1915-18. State Archives. Small photo a Pavesi Tolotti type B tractor. Author Archive.

PAVESI P4 TRACTOR - ITALY 1922-1936

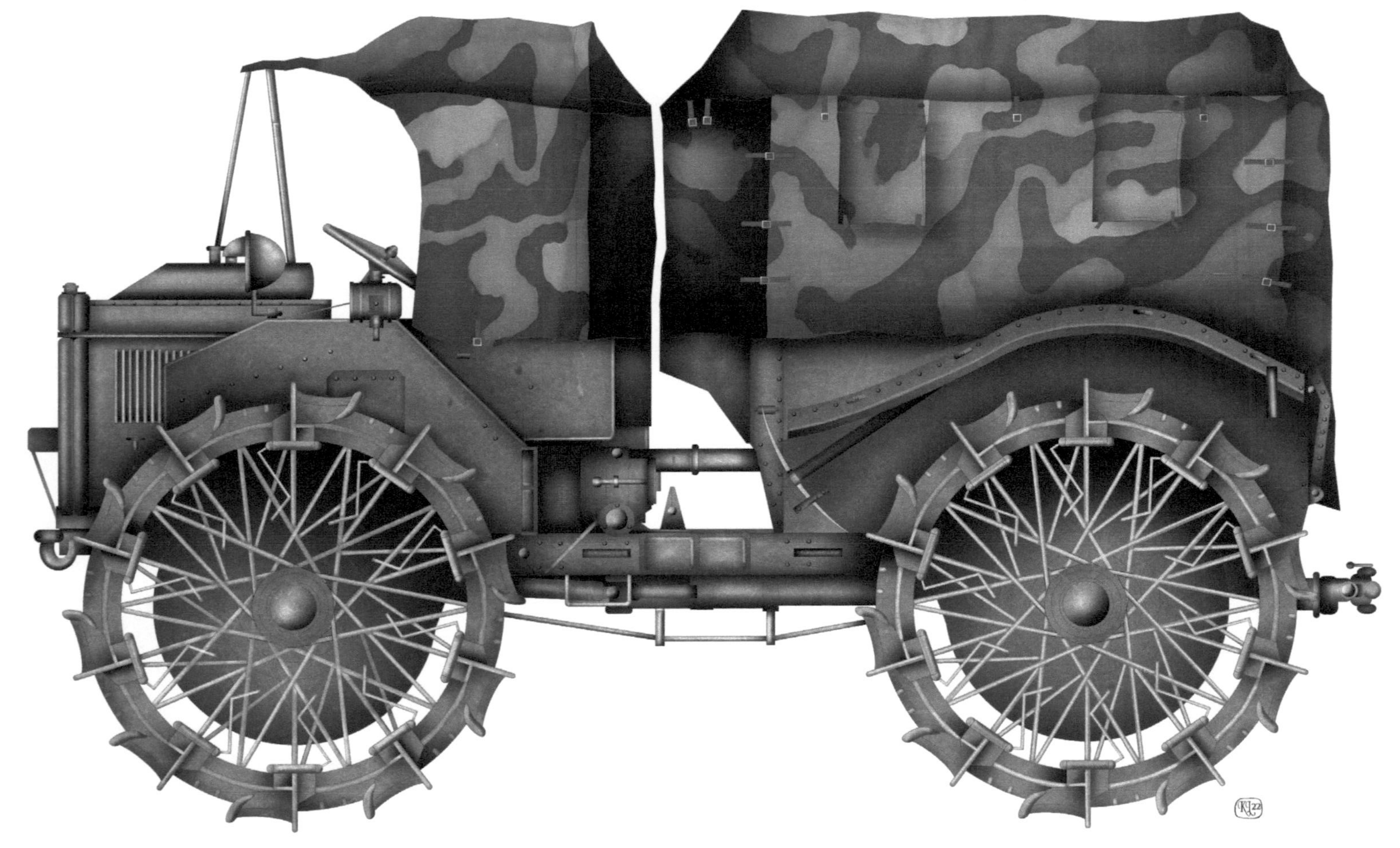

PAVESI P4 TRACTOR

The Pavesi P4 was born as an innovative and experimental agricultural tractor and was designed by Ugo Pavesi from Novara, which gave the vehicle its name. The Royal Army General Staff soon realised its potential and acquired it as an artillery tractor.

It was the first Italian four-wheel-drive tractor and among the first in the world, presenting other innovative and futuristic solutions, such as large wheels of equal diameter and the double articulated frame. The military version was an immediate success. The Regio Esercito selected the 'Pavesi P4/100' version as a heavy artillery tractor in 1923. The request from the Ministry of War spoke of a 'tractor with total adhesion for towing heavy artillery': the Pavesi beat off competition from all others presented by Fiat and Ansaldo. The chosen model was slightly modified and lengthened compared to the agricultural version. The army ordered 1,000 examples, but Pavesi had great difficulty fulfilling this order and the production licence for the artillery tractor was sold to Fiat and its subsidiary Società Piemontese Automobili (SPA). In 1931 the tractor was further improved with the launch of the 'Mod. 30', followed in 1934 by the 'Mod. 30A'.

The vehicle was assigned to the units in the ratio of five units per battery, four of which were for towing pieces and one in reserve. It had its baptism of fire as usual in the AOI where 136 examples were sent, and later another 82 examples in the Spanish Civil War with the Volunteer Troops Corps. During the Second World War, the Pavesi was still in the Army Corps artillery towing the 105/28, 105/32, 149/12 Mod. 14, Škoda 15 cm Vz. 1914, 149/19 Mod. 1937 and for towing the 75/46 C.A. Mod. 1934 anti-aircraft piece. Its use was widespread, although its low speed was beginning to make it obsolete. Nevertheless, it was used on all fronts, until it was replaced in 1942 on the assembly lines and battlefield by the SPA TM40. The tractor was also successful abroad, gaining orders even in the UK where it was produced under licence in 1929. Greece ordered 224 Mod. 30A tractors in 1935 which, ironically, were later used against Italian troops on the border with Albania. Hungary, Sweden, Finland and Bulgaria were other customers. In Spain, after the Civil War, it remained in service with Franco's army. Of course, after 8 September it was also employed by the Germans, who named it Radschlepper Pavesi Typ P 40-100 (i).

SPECIFICATIONS:	
Entry into service	1919-1942
Full load weight	5.600 kg
Chassis length	3,5 metres
Power	40/57 hp
Displacement	4700
Vehicle width	1,9 metres
Maximum speed	11/20 km/h
Autonomy	180 km
Number of parts available in 1940	N.A.

◼ SPECIFICATIONS

The artillery tractor had open bodies on the two chassis, with large mudguards. The front chassis housed an open body with a removable canvas cover, and at the front it mounted the engine. The bodywork of the rear chassis was more extensively modified; the cabin housed six seats for crew in the Mod. 26 and four in the Mod. 30, which, folded down, left a load compartment of 1000 or 2000 kg in the two models respectively. The body could also be covered with a waterproof tarpaulin on a removable bowed frame. The large mudguards, could also accommodate crew luggage or other materials. The large wheels with solid rubber tyres and folding paddles attached to the inner wheels were excellent on rough Italian terrain but sank on the sandy, soft soils of the colonies; thus in 1937 Pirelli 'Green Seal' tyres were adopted on Mod. 30 and 30A.

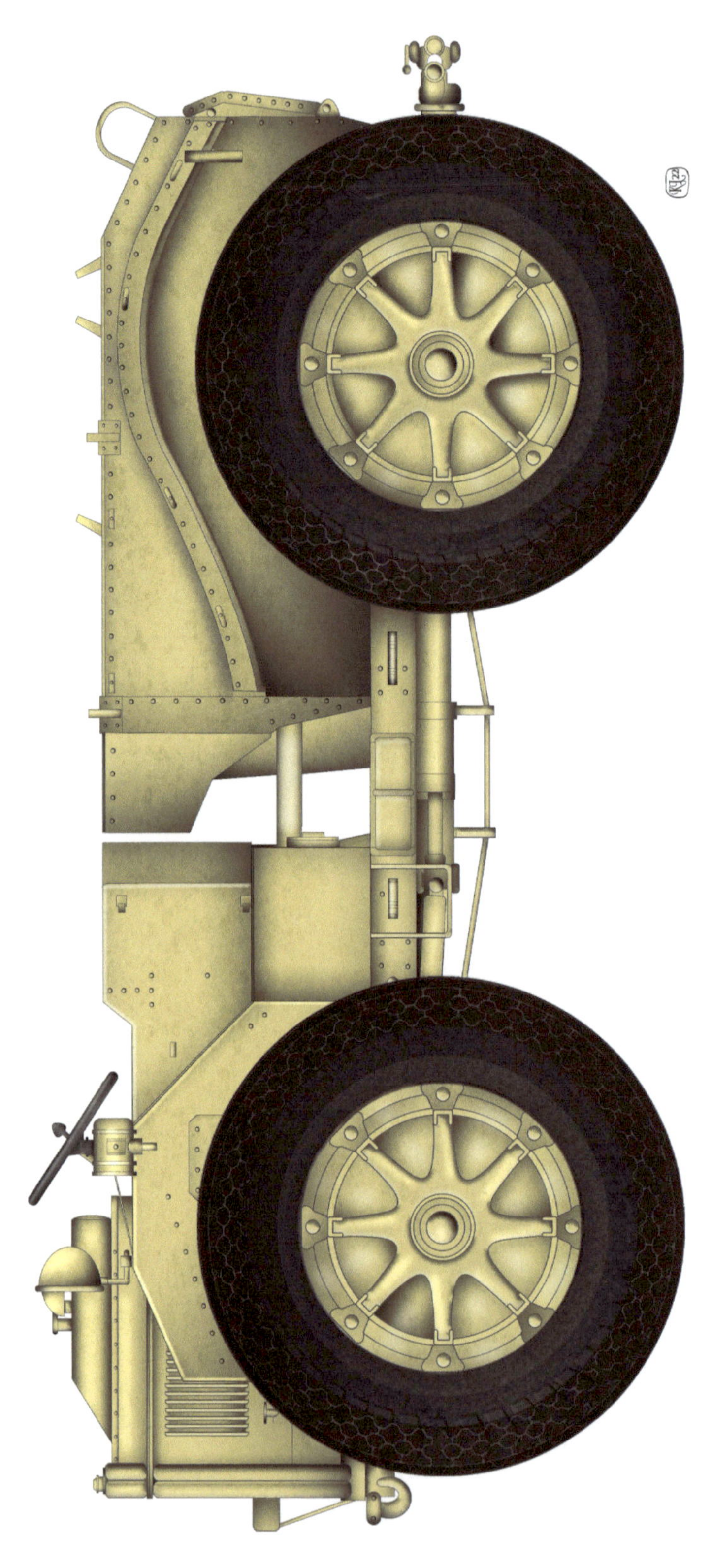

▲ Above a Pavesi P4 in AOI with a 149/35 in tow. Author archive.

► On the right HM the King visiting the front, two Pavesi with cannons in tow can be seen. State Archives.

▼ Below a Pavesi tractor towing a 105-28 on the African front between Tripoli and Homs. State Archives.

BIBLIOGRAPHY

- Balocco R. – *Fanti ed Artiglieri* – Manualetti di Tecnica Militare, Fascicolo XXI, dic. 1934
- Barlozzetti U. & Alberto Pirella *Mezzi dell'Esercito Italiano 1935-45*, Editoriale Olimpia, 1986.
- Benussi G. *Autocannoni, autoblinde e veicoli speciali del regio esercito Italiano nella prima guerra mondiale.* Integest Milano 1973.
- Bovi L, Antonio e Andrea Talillo. *Semoventi da 47/32, 90/53 e 75/18 in Sicilia.* Ediz. illustrata - Ardite edizioni 2021. Italia
- Cappellano F. – *Le artiglierie del regio esercito nella seconda guerra mondiale*, Albertelli, 1998
- Cappellano F. *Mortai del Regio esercito* Storia militare agosto 1997
- Ceva L., Curami A. – *La meccanizzazione dell'esercito italiano dalle origini al 1943* – Stato Maggiore Esercito, Ufficio Storico, 1994
- Chiappa E., *CTV - il corpo truppe volontarie italiano durante la guerra civile spagnola*, 2003 EMI.
- COMITATO PER LA STORIA DELL'ARTIGLIERIA, *Storia dell'artiglieria italiana*, vol. XVI, 1955
- Cucut C. - *Le forze armate della RSI* –Gruppo Modellistica Trentino, 2005
- Cucut C. *Le artiglierie delle forze armate della Repubblica sociale italiana.* Soldiershop ottobre 2020
- De Rosa Gabriele *Storia dell'Ansaldo 6. Dall'IRI alla guerra 1930-1945*, Gius. Laterza & Figli, 1999.
- Favagrossa C. – *Perché perdemmo la guerra* – Rizzoli, 1946
- Finazzer E. *Guida alle artiglierie italiane nella seconda guerra mondiale, 1940-1945. Regio esercito italiano, Repubblica Sociale Italiana, esercito cobelligerante.* IS Genova 2020.
- Finazzer E. *Le Artiglierie del regio esercito nella seconda guerra mondiale.* Soldiershop 2017.
- Finazzer E & Riccio R. *Italian Artillery of the Second World War.* Mushroom 2015.
- Grandi F., *Dati sommari sulle artiglierie in servizio e sul tiro*, Ed. fuori commercio, 1934.
- Grandi F., *Le armi e le artiglierie in servizio*, Ed. fuori commercio, 1938.
- Guglielmi Daniele *Semoventi M41 & M42*. Armor Photogallery -Broncos (in inglese)
- Montanari M.– *L'esercito italiano alla vigilia della 2ª Guerra Mondiale* – Stato Maggiore Esercito, Ufficio Storico, 1975
- Pergher C. – *Le macchine di Pavesi* – Gruppo Modellistico Trentino, 2002
- Pignato N. – *L'obice da 149/19 OTO 1937* – Storia Militare n. 150, marzo 2006
- Pignato N. - *Artiglierie e automezzi dell'esercito italiano nella Seconda guerra mondiale.* Albertelli editore 1972
- Pignato N. Cappellano F. – *L'obice da 210/22 mod. 35* – Storia Militare n. 171, gennaio 2008
- Pignato N. – *Il 105/28 del Regio Esercito* – Storia Militare n. 182, novembre 2008
- Pignato N. – *L'ultimo 75 dell'artiglieria italiana* – Storia Militare n. 188, maggio 2009
- Pignato N. – *Un "pezzo da 90"* – Storia Militare n. 201, giugno 2010
- Pignato, N. *Semovente da 75/18 : tecnica e storia del primo semovente italiano.* (2010).Parma: Albertelli.
- Raudino S. e Stefanelli E. – *Storia dell'artiglieria italiana*, parte V – voll. XV e XVI - Rivista d'artiglieria e genio 1953 - 1955
- Rovighi A. – F. Stefani, *La partecipazione italiana alla guerra civile spagnola*, USSME, 1992.
- Tonoli M. e F. Corsetti *Skodas Gebirgskanone Model 15 1915-1964* – Itinera Progetti (2013).

PUBLISHED TITLES

TWE-006 EN